The Cure for Career Quicksand

BY REAGAN CANNON

Reagan
Cannon

I dedicate this book to my loving husband.

Thank you for putting up with me
and believing in me all these years.

WHAT'S IN THIS BOOK?

LONG-TERM VIEW

EVERY MISTAKE MATTERS

DEAR
FELLOW
JOURNEYMAN

You are sitting in a cubical at 8 p.m., wondering why you are still working instead of having a drink with your friends or why you aren't home spending time with your family. But, this is the third (or fourth, or fifth or I've stopped counting) job in your career, and you are determined to make it work.

I am not a doctor, but I think I can safely diagnose you with the disease that plagued me and plagues so many Americans: "Career Quicksand Disease." Here are the symptoms:

- Itching and burning desire for something new
- Increased coffee cup sizes (or wine glasses)
- Nausea and anxiety every Sunday night
- Extended lengths of boredom lasting longer than 4 hours

You do a good job each day, but know that if you had a little more inspiration you could turn in even better work. It appears the harder you work, the faster you paddle, the deeper and deeper you sink. Worst of all, there is an overwhelming sense of feeling stuck.

Whether this describes you now, or you just want to take steps to make sure it never does, this book is for you. It has 21 chapters of insights that will help you take your eyes off of the time flashing on your phone and put them squarely on a sound, strategic, thoughtful plan for your career. It is an actionable approach to treating your symptoms and getting you on the road to career recovery.

Some of these strategies involve more of a physical change such as a change in your surroundings. Others involve choices regarding your education, or role. Other strategies might involve a little change to the man or woman you see in the mirror each day.

Don't forget: There is no "easy" button when it comes to career success. Find a way to use today to invest in tomorrow. In fact, with the right investments, you can actually accelerate your career. Use a positive attitude, great people skills, a willingness to take proactive steps, a long-term career plan and most importantly, the ability to learn from mistakes, to give you a competitive edge. Eventually, you will be the one buying that round of drinks for your friends or grilling a steak in your backyard at 5:30. Cheers!

Your Fellow Journeyman,

Reagan

ALLOW
ME TO
INTRODUCE
MYSELF

If you are going to spend the next 21 chapters with me, I figured you might want to know how it all got started.

My professional career began like most 11-year olds: babysitting. But I was not like every other babysitter. I understood differentiation and branding from a young age. My first marketing campaign was when I was 11, and it involved me writing all my qualifications on notecards and making copies at the local library. I then did a mail drop by hand in my neighborhood. I had a 2% response on my campaign, with two phone calls, well above the 1% industry standard for direct mail. What made it more impressive is that I advertised myself as a great "babbysitter." Too bad notecards didn't have spell check or I might have had an even larger response to my efforts.

My career then made the typical progression to "teenager who works at clothing store in mall." Again, I took the path less traveled and broke every sales record at my store. I made the nationally-ranked list of sellers for my large retail chain. When asked by my district manager how I was so successful,

I documented my best practices and labeled them: "Reagan's Rules." It contained sophisticated sales tips like, "Ask the customer her favorite color, and then show her all the clothes in that color." Worked like a charm.

In college, I had three goals for when I graduated. I wanted a job with a big company. I wanted to make $40K. And I wanted a Volkswagen Cabriolet. I am happy to report that I achieved all 3. Although, had I known my first job out of college would not be in Southern California, but in Chicago, I might have skipped buying a convertible. (I think I was the only crazy person in Chicago who "dropped the top" as soon as the weather even flirted with 50 degrees.)

Then came my professional life. The first 10 years of my career were your typical roller coaster ride. I had moments of thrilling success and moments of total defeat. I made some great decisions and some terrible mistakes. I used a lot of spell check, but sometimes the content of my message was so poor, it didn't even matter. I regret a grand total of none of my decisions and treasure what I learned from each and every experience.

WORK
THIS
BOOK

Now, let's get down to business and talk about how to make this book work for you. It is broken into 5 sections. Each collection of stories represents an area of your career that can easily become "career quicksand."

Every chapter will start out with my own personal story. Names have been changed, of course, to protect the innocent people who got stuck working with me. However, the lessons I share are 100% authentic.

You can choose to read this book a few different ways:

Old School:
There is always the traditional cover-to-cover method (never knock an old stand by).

Daily Nuggets:
There is also the daily method where you read a chapter each day. There are 21 chapters and about that many work days in a month. So, if you choose, you can read and reflect on one each day, and scratch down your personal learnings in the

margin, post them on your preferred method of social media, or just call your mom and assure her you are actually still learning something in life.

Group Thinking:

You can also read this book as a group. Find a couple of friends and decide you want to hash out the principles and keep away the quicksand together. More information can be found at the end of the book about my free online "group guide" and how to divide the book up into weekly discussions.

Look for a "Reagan's Rule" at the end of each chapter. This is the quick summary, in 2 sentences or less, of a rule that I try and live by. After each rule, there is a set of thought provoking questions that can help you put this lesson into practice in your life.

As you are reading the book, pay close attention to the chapters that resonate with you. Look for "aha" moments that really make you think. Be especially aware of the pesky chapters that bother you. Sometimes when something stings, it means it has hit on a nerve. Earmark those and ask a trusted friend why the story might be hitting close to home.

Any way you read this book, have fun, and join me on the wild ride that is my life. Get ready to turn my career stories into lessons for yours!

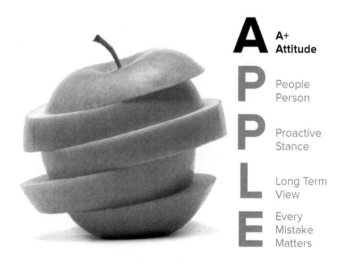

A A+
Attitude

P People
Person

P Proactive
Stance

L Long Term
View

E Every
Mistake
Matters

A+
ATTITUDE

Attitude is the seed of your career.
Plant it well, and you have an oak tree.
Plant it wrong, and you have a weed.

1 | THE BIG A

It was bumper-to-bumper on the freeway. I knew LA traffic was bad because I grew up in Southern California, but I had never quite experienced it like this. I had just changed jobs and was commuting to work for the first time. I thought I had been clever by leaving at 6:45 a.m. My new boss was flying into town and was expecting me to let him into the office for our meeting. I sat helpless, looking at my car clock as it displayed 7:30am in bright green. I wasn't even half way to my office.

When I finally arrived at 9:00 a.m., I realized that I had bitten off a little more than I'd expected with this commute. I knew it was 48 miles on paper, but the reality was daily monster traffic snares on the dreaded 10 freeway. I sat in my office, listening to my new boss tell me how he waited outside for 30 minutes, before someone else finally showed up to let him in. (Insert my wanting to climb under the table, not to mention making a fabulous first impression...ughhh.)

After he left, I immediately wanted to call my husband, burst into tears, and feel nice and sorry for myself. Instead, I sat in my office and made an intentional decision; I would NEVER complain about my commute. I had wanted this opportunity, and I was so excited to be in marketing. I told myself that I would investigate public transportation, leave earlier, join a gym to wait out traffic, or do whatever else it took to not lose my mind. For the almost five years I made the commute, I complained less than the digits on my left hand. It was with a "make it work" attitude that I was able to tame my beast of a commute.

LESSON LEARNED

I remember being 10 years old and complaining to my mom that I was bored. She would say, "Well, with that attitude, of course you're bored." She was annoying, but she was right. When you think you are bored, you are. When you think you are miserable, you are. A bad attitude has a way of becoming a self-fulfilling prophecy. The more you complain, the more you believe your complaints. A complaint festers into a bad mood and a bad mood into a bad attitude. Then your bad attitude ruins everything else around you.

Conversely, you can stave off this cycle with the decision to have a good attitude. It is not going to happen naturally. You can't fall into a good attitude; it takes work. Everything around you wants you to be discontented. Commercials are telling you that you need this or that if you want to be happy. News is barely even watchable now because it gains ratings by telling you everything that is dangerous, awful and toxic. So, if you want to have a positive disposition, you have to start out by saying you want it and then work at it every day.

Here are a few tips to help you keep your attitude positive. First, practice gratitude. Right now, take out a piece of paper and write down 15 things you are grateful for; bet you come up with 20. We have so much we are blessed with but we rarely stop to contemplate the bounty. Naysayers claim that gratefulness doesn't change your surroundings. It does however change the way you see them.

Secondly, don't allow yourself to get sucked into "complainy" conversations. You know what I'm talking about. You're sitting around with co-workers and systematically taking down one colleague after another. In the work place, this happens subtly. First, it's your boss calling a bunch of pointless meetings. Then it's the HR guy with all of his annoying company policies. Then it's those nut-jobs in shipping! Next thing you know, you're barreling down the poor me highway without a seatbelt or airbags. And then finally, you're in a full-blown funk, thinking, "Why do I even work for this stupid place and these stupid people?" A spark of dissatisfaction can grow like wildfire. Stomp out these sparks of conversation before they grow. Only you can prevent discontentment fires.

Lastly, you need to laugh a lot. If you want to stay positive, find a way to laugh at whatever outrageous situation you find yourself in. When I was commuting 4 hours a day, I would always find time to people-watch in Union Station. I couldn't beat it for entertainment – street performers, exasperated parents, men in suits running full speed to catch the 6:00 train... there was so much humanity to entertain me if I took the time to observe. And, I can only imagine what all the other observers thought when they saw me – dressed in a fancy suit, every hair perfectly in place, make-up to the nines... and flip-flops. Four hours wearing heels on the bus? I don't think so!

There are very few things that matter as much as, or are as fundamental as the big A, because it impacts every other aspect of your career and your life.

Reagan's RULE

The right attitude is the key to your success.

PUTTING IT TO WORK

Describe a difficult situation that you were able to deal with because you consciously decided to cultivate a good attitude. How did your improved attitude help you cope?

Who is the most "complainy" person you know? How do you feel after you've been with this person?

Think of a time that was "#serious" in the moment but now you look back and laugh at yourself. How can you take steps to laugh in the moment and change your attitude in real time?

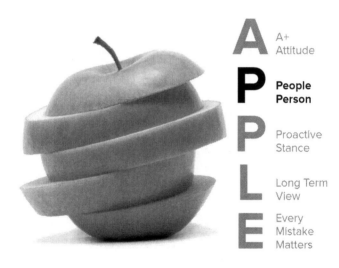

A A+
Attitude

P **People**
Person

P Proactive
Stance

L Long Term
View

E Every
Mistake
Matters

PEOPLE PERSON

The people you work for, with, or lead, can make or break your success. It is never all about you.

CHAPTER

2 | **DON'T JUDGE A BOSS BY HER HANDBAG**

Not only was she well dressed in her black Chanel jacket, she had the most amazing black Prada handbag. Trust me – it was the real thing, definitely not a knock off. She was my new boss, Amanda, and beyond the impeccable wardrobe and immaculate grooming, her mere presence was enough to make me feel more than a tad insecure. She was tiny, but she carried a big punch. She was an entertainment-marketing expert, and I barely knew how to spell movie premiere. She took the wheel and put her foot firmly on the accelerator. She had big ideas, and she wasn't afraid to speak her mind.

Before this marketing role, I had been in front line positions. These were customer-facing jobs where the boss was very engaged, patient and involved in my work. Amanda came from a very different environment – actually she came from another planet when it came to management. She said things to me like, "If I have to do your job, then why are you here?" She demanded that a first draft of any report or presentation be near final. Wow!

This was new to me. I thought, "Come on, let me just put some thoughts on paper and get your guidance before I do all this work." That would be a "no go" situation.

I also learned the hard way that she lived and died by her Outlook calendar. I once walked into her office, and she looked at me a little flustered. Finally, she said, "Hey Reagan, I don't have you on my calendar right now." OK. I guess I will schedule something with you and come back...

At first glance, Amanda looked like a terrible mismatch for me. How on earth could I navigate this situation? Then, one day, I realized something – Amanda was everything I was not. She had skills that I had not yet acquired. She knew how to get her people to take ownership of their work, where I usually did work for people if I thought I could do it faster. She demanded perfection, where I often let things slide. She was organized and used every drop of her day, where I was usually a socializer who lost countless hours because I didn't plan my time.

The more I observed and copied her, the better I got at time management, setting high expectations and learning to delegate. I didn't give up who I was, but I stole every single trick she had up her designer jacket sleeve. In the four years I worked for her, I developed skills I never thought possible. It was a transformation and evolution that would serve me well for the rest of my career...and, yes, I did eventually upgrade my handbag.

LESSON LEARNED

The old saying that, "you can learn from any boss," is really true. Every boss teaches you some qualities you can apply to your own leadership style. Even the worst bosses teach you what not to do.

Good bosses can teach you a lot and can come in lots of different flavors. The really charismatic ones are engaging, and they pull you in with their charm. They energize you and inspire you to turn in great work. The really smart bosses challenge your thinking and open your mind to new ideas. They make you count your words and think through your ideas before you speak (which is nearly impossible for an extrovert like me).

The really tough bosses are the ones who can get a bad rap. They demand perfection from you. You feel you can't do enough, and they constantly want more. Then, just when you feel like you can't give any more, they hand you a little flash of confidence to keep you going. They select you for a special project. They stop in one day and thank you personally for the report you stayed late to perfect. They fight for you when you are stuck without the resources you need to finish a project. You see that they are just as demanding of everyone else as they are of you. It's under these tough bosses, that you wake up one day and realize you have turned in the best work of your career.

I have also found in my career that the chances of clicking with bosses can be greatly improved by learning how to appropriately manage them. I know that sounds a little backwards, but it is true. Each leader has their own style of communication. If you insist on speaking French and they are speaking German, then you are going to constantly misunderstand each other. The best way to avoid this is to utilize a concept referred to as "mirroring." If your boss is super structured, make sure you emulate that structure in your e-mails and meeting agendas. If your boss likes to be more relational, then build time into your meetings where you can connect personally. Adjusting your style to their style helps you learn from and work well with a range of personalities.

One of the most popular trends in the workplace today is for supervisors to have an open door policy. You know, the one where they say, "Hey, I want to hear what you really think. Come on in." Let me translate that for you, since I am fluent in manager-speak. The real meaning of this is, "I want to hear what you have to say in the right place, at the right time and in the right context." I have foolishly tried to argue with a boss in front of the entire team and found this open door policy was a door slammed in my face. A leader can benefit tremendously from getting insight and honest opinions. Just be smart about what should happen behind closed doors and what should happen out on the floor. This is critical to having a good relationship with your boss versus one that is constantly under strain.

The net of all these lessons is this – don't judge a manager by your first few interactions. As you learn and adjust to your boss over a period of time, you can dramatically improve that relationship. Plus, you might find that the toughest boss you work for, might actually change your life.

Reagan's RULE

Don't be quick to write off a boss based on your first impressions. Adjust your style to meet theirs, so you can work with and learn from any kind of supervisor.

PUTTING IT TO WORK

Who is the best boss you've ever had? Why?

How are you different, having had a leader like this?

Describe a **Lesson Learned** from a poor boss and how it affects your leadership style.

Is there anything you can be doing or adjusting in your style to better communicate with your current boss?

CHAPTER

3

ADULTS ARE NOT THAT DIFFERENT THAN KIDS

At one turning point in my career, I became a Sales Manager. I was coming into an office with another Sales Manager, who was to be my peer and equal. She was very experienced and very used to running the show. Let's call her Competitive Carla.

Unfortunately, she was only introduced to me as Carla. Like every young, naive pup, I was excited to learn from her and had visions of our being fast friends – bringing each other coffees in the mornings, maybe drinks after work to help decompress. Turned out she was not excited in return. As a matter of fact, she did a little (actually a lot) of strategic team rearranging before I even arrived! The result: she had all the high performers on her team, and I had all the misfit toys. Yes, I'm sure you can paint a picture: new, low performing, and high maintenance. We were a rag tag group that I was tasked with making into a unified and productive team. Yeah....

So a little more on Carla...she was a private person and didn't like to involve me in a lot of the office decisions. Because she was experienced and had cred, and I was new and had none, this did not bode well for my Sales Manager deployment. I heard rumors that she had conversations about my "crazy" leadership style behind my back with my own team members. It was junior high all over again!

To my face, Miss Competitive Carla was nothing short of Susie Sugarplum. But there were crazy vibes in the office. It wasn't that there were a lot of overt things she would do or say, to me at least. It was much more subtle. Carla was not an evil person. She was a person fiercely protecting her space and her way of doing things. She was the queen of this roost, and she was not interested in giving an inch to the new girl.

At the end of that rotation, I had to admit that I'd learned a lot from my peer, just not the lessons I was expecting. I learned the hard way that not all adults are members of my fan club, and it is best if I stop acting as if they are.

LESSON LEARNED

When you are growing up, adults are usually on your side. They are coaching you, teaching you, or driving you somewhere. Then, at some point along the way, you move from "kid" to "competition." You start vying for the same opportunities, raises, and eventually, promotions. This change happens fast, and you don't always see it coming when you start your career.

The secret weapon in dealing with this is a healthy dose of reality. You want to make sure you build trust with the RIGHT people. Ronald Reagan once said, "Trust, but verify." Ronnie was onto something. It is important to verify peoples' motives through observation, over a length of time. So watch and listen carefully. Do they always make promises but rarely follow through? Or promise everything to everyone? Do they ask you to share your intimate thoughts on everything but never share their true feelings on anything? Take all these clues into account to make a true assessment.

Once you have observed someone's behavior and trustworthiness, you have to go with your instinct. I get a feeling when I meet people if they are going to be close compadres at work. The more I get to know them, the more I watch them in action, the more I trust them. A trusted friend at work can be invaluable. He or she can become the person you can confide in, vent safely to, and trust to get you through the tough points in your career. In fact, I often make matching BFF bracelets and share my snack packs with them; I guess not all childish behavior is bad.

Reagan's RULE

The office is not your personal fan club. Observe actions over time and build trust with the right people who are in your corner.

PUTTING IT TO WORK

Who is your BFF at work? How long did it take you to build a trusting relationship with this person?

Who did you mistakenly trust was in your corner only to find out they were not? Looking back now, were there any warning signs you missed?

What are three behaviors you can look for, in order to build trust with someone?

CHAPTER

4 | **THE BOSS SAID SO**

Somehow I found myself in a position of power. I was the Chief of Staff for Joyce Renner, a very important leader at my company. She was brought into the organization to infuse fresh energy and leadership. That also meant she was putting forward ideas that were very different from the status quo. It meant a lot of change for people who had been doing things "the right way" for a very long time.

As her Chief of Staff, I took on several projects to help perpetuate her initiatives. I remember vividly the first few calls with Joyce's extended support team — the awkward silences as I asked my peers to change processes they had grown so accustomed to. "Hey guys, thanks for joining the call today. We are going to discuss changing all the reporting." (Insert sound of crickets chirping...)

Finally, someone brave enough would ask why we were making these changes. It would have been really easy to say, "because Joyce said so." But I held myself in check, and instead, started to explain Joyce's thought process. I gave the team a sneak peek into her vision and helped them see why these changes were critical to moving the team and the organization forward. This didn't always work, but the majority of employees appreciated the explanation. It made them feel part of her vision, instead of feeling like it was an assault on their way of life. Some even said it was the first time someone in a leadership role had taken the time to paint a picture of the overall plan, rather than simply giving orders.

The changes that Joyce had in mind were broad and far-reaching. So over time, I took initiative to get to know the key players throughout our organization. I preemptively reached out, before an actual action item was initiated, because I could tell where she was moving and where I would need help soon. After several weeks, I found that trust was building, and that people not only believed in Joyce's vision but had grown to trust me. My boss may have been the one asking for the change, but I was the one they were willing to work for to get it done.

LESSON LEARNED

People love their moms, yet they still hate being told, "because mom said so." It may cause children to comply, but it does not cause them to engage or understand. Employees are no different. We all have a reporting structure that tells us what we have to do. What people want is to feel inspired by a vision, understand the thought process behind the activity or change, and not feel forced to simply comply.

At some point in your career, you might find yourself in a position of power. Let's say for example, you were selected to manage a team, and you are by far the least experienced person on the team. Perhaps, you find yourself in charge of a growing project others want to be a part of. Or, you might be like me and have the ear of a very important executive. Whatever power you find yourself holding, be very careful how you use it.

People tend to do two things with power. The first is they easily give it away. They defer to too many people and want to be overly inclusive in order to maintain friendships and be liked. The result is that leaders are often taken advantage of, not listened to or respected.

The second mistake is the total opposite. Leaders frequently hold onto their new power too tightly. They have a bright, shiny object, and they are not going to share. They keep things secret from everyone and say things like, "I can't tell you," or, "You are not on the core team, so you wouldn't understand, " or, "You need to get this done for our boss; just trust me."

The right balance is to bring people along with your power. Don't rely on your power to be the reason people will help you or support you. Treat everyone with respect and build individual relationships with all levels within your org, regardless of title. Trust me on this – your relationship with the temp in shipping may be as critical as your relationship with the big boss, when you want to move an initiative forward. Remember that the frontline workers in your organization are often the very people who can fuel your success. They see the blind spots in your plan because they know exactly how it will impact the customer or the greater employee base. Create forums, like focus groups, where you can get many angles on a plan. Then allow their feedback to have a seat at the table when you are making decisions.

When working with a group on a project, share generously the pieces of the story that are important to your various stakeholders. Then set clear expectations regarding what needs to be done and make sure your team moves together. There may be a time and place when you have met enough resistance to say, "The boss said so," but always use that as a last resort.

Reagan's RULE

Don't name drop to get things done. Build relationships so your colleagues will want to get things done for you.

PUTTING IT TO WORK

Describe a situation where you were asked to change a process and didn't understand the reasoning.

How did you feel about the change and the person delivering the order?

How would you have handled the situation if you'd been in charge?

CHAPTER

5

CLEAN UP ON AISLE 5

All their eyes followed Lisa as she walked past me, pulled out a chair and sat at the conference room table. On this particular morning, I had a team meeting with my service reps at the start of our shift. Since Lisa was late, she walked directly into the conference room without clocking in. That meant I was responsible for logging her start time and her tardy. This was not her first tardy. In fact, it was number 15. You might think, "Wow, the company has a lenient tardy policy." Truth is, this was way over the limit. In a union environment that was governed by rules and contracts, this situation was controversial, to say the least. Lisa was a single mother with four children. She had a lot of challenges getting to work, so we tried to be flexible. However, she had been warned that one additional tardy would mean the end of her employment.

After the meeting, as required, I sent a note to Janelle. She was my attendance manager and I was obliged to let her know that Lisa had arrived at 8:07 a.m. As expected, a few hours later, Janelle came upstairs, union steward in tow. This was not a good sign, since the union must be present for terminations. She walked over to my desk, looked me straight in the eyes and said, "Are you sure Lisa was late this morning? It is really important that you validate your e-mail."

This was one of those time-stands-still moments. If I say, "Yes," Lisa loses her job, and I have to live with the thought of her being unable to support her family. On the other hand, if I lie, I lose credibility with my entire team. They all saw her walk in late. They all know her situation. And they are all tired of her being treated differently.

This gut-wrenching scenario wasn't exactly covered in my Leadership 101 course in college. I made my tough decision, sat up, and clearly and emphatically said, "Yes, I am sure."

LESSON LEARNED

Everyone dreams about promotions and says things like, "When I run this place, I am going to put real creamer in the break room." We think of it as an ideal, but the reality of being a leader is very different. If you are one of those "go getters" who wants to be promoted to management, you need to understand some hard truths about leadership.

First, leading people will provide you with moments of total elation and fulfillment. People can be inspired, lifted up, developed and motivated to great success. They can climb huge mountains, and you can be their Sherpa. It is amazing to come into work and see someone achieve something he or she never thought possible because of some coaching or advice you delivered. These are the moments that motivate you to come to work every day, not just the paycheck.

The second thing you need to know is that these are people you are leading, which means you'll have frustrating moments and difficult decisions to make. People have lives, personal issues and make really poor decisions. They will have bad days. They will cry on your desk. They will sleep with someone in the office. It happens. And if you are the big boss in charge, you have to deal with all of it.

Some managers try to avoid these situations, claiming it's not part of the job. They say things like, "I am here to do a job, not deal with personal issues." Wrong! The job is to lead your people, and that means you have to engage them. You have to referee, you have to counsel, you have to listen, and sometimes you have to make swift and unpopular decisions.

Great leaders understand that there is a human being behind that employee ID number. When someone has brought personal "junk" to the workplace, it can sit and fester like a gigantic, fat elephant in the room. It hurts the employee and the team. You are all in the foxhole together, and a wounded soldier slows the entire platoon.

Leaders who have honed their interpersonal skills turn these situations into opportunities to strengthen their relationships with the employee and ultimately the team. They handle each situation, head on, with grace and confidence.

There are a lot of messes when it comes to leading people, so get out the mop and get down to aisle 5 to clean them up. It might just be the most rewarding thing you do.

Managing humans is messy. But if done with heart, it can be the most rewarding part of your career.

PUTTING IT TO WORK

Give an example of a time where a co-worker brought personal issues to work, and a manager did not handle it well. What could they have done differently to help the employee and the team?

Now, describe a current situation where someone's personal drama is becoming a huge distraction and slowing down the team's performance. What can you do to improve the situation? (Hint: head in the sand is not a strategy).

Are there any personal situations you have that are creeping their way onto the job? Is there something you can do to mitigate their negative impact?

6 | THE ROPE

It was my turn to manage an intern as part of our 6-month accelerated leadership program. I was a graduate of this very program, so I was confident I had a handle on what was involved. As the typical Type A personality, I was determined to be the best manager of all time. After all, the participants rated me at the end of the rotation.

This was a crazy-busy time in my career. I had a big marketing job and was responsible for bringing in over $100M in revenue and had massive targets for growth. Bottom line — I had a lot on my plate and was looking to delegate. I started doling out smaller campaigns and tasks so that "Adam the Intern" could get his feet wet. I could tell that this was not the thrilling marketing rotation he'd expected. When he heard "entertainment marketing," he was waiting for the movie stars to jump out of supply closets, just like ESPN commercials. Instead, he was proofreading legal text on a direct mail piece.

So, I decided that my task was to inspire and empower Adam. Even though he hadn't shown a ton of promise, I would take a leap and throw him a bone. In fact, I threw him a really big bone. I told Adam that he would be quarterbacking the next pay-per-view fight campaign, solo! It featured a big name boxer and would bring in an excess of a million dollars. I thought these flashy names and figures would surely motivate him.

I gave Adam total freedom to design the entire marketing campaign. If he had a clever social media idea (isn't everyone under 30 a social media expert?), he could run with it. If he thought a direct mail piece would work, I would fund it. I even told him that he could dream-up an interactive video for an e-mail blast, and we would do it. What more could he want?

A week later we got back together, and he turned in a campaign with:

- A blurb on our Facebook page

- A direct mail piece

- An e-mail with a video embedded

What?! I paused after reading this plan. "So Adam," I finally got out, "this is your plan? I thought you wanted more ownership and more responsibility to create something original. These are the very same ideas we discussed a week ago."

His response was classic for an MBA intern, "Yeah Reagan, it's just that I really want to be more strategic." He was so busy posting selfies on Instagram that he didn't notice I had given him a very strategic project! I think what he really meant was he didn't want to do the work associated with the campaign. I had given him the responsibility he had asked for, and he hung himself with it.

LESSON LEARNED

Nobody says, "I really want to be micromanaged and constricted. I want you to shoot down all my ideas and frustrate me." So, as a good boss, you should always have a healthy paranoia that you are stifling people's creativity. You hire people because they have talent. It is important that you give them the room to use that talent. But, as a leader, it gets challenging to understand when and how much to let loose of the reins.

If you are a high performer, you take pride and ownership in your work. You probably want the fence outline of the corral, and then you want to be able to trot and gallop freely in the context of your job. You don't need micromanagement, and you never need to be "sat on" to do your work.

So, when high performers move to management, the fact that employees need motivation to do a job is confusing. These new managers say or think things like, "Don't these employees want to do a good job?" and, "Don't they understand their names are on their work?" Yes, they understand. They just don't care. Or they are not motivated by freedom. Or maybe, they think they like freedom, but they find they cannot handle it.

The best approach to becoming a successful manager is to learn to let the leash out slowly. My husband was a teacher for many years. His approach was to start each new school year being really tough. Then as the year progressed, he could let loose more and more, as the kids proved themselves.

I wish that corporate America was more sophisticated than his sixth graders, but the same rule applies. Start with structured parameters and smaller tasks. Don't listen to comments such as, "I rarely have to be managed," or, "I am self-motivated." Make your employees prove themselves. If they do in short order, you can let go sooner. If they struggle, you can keep the controls and guide strongly. Don't let the rope out so fast they tie themselves up in knots and fail.

Reagan's RULE

If you give people too much rope, too quickly, they may hang themselves with it! Release responsibility as they earn it.

PUTTING IT TO WORK

Describe a work situation where you felt underutilized. Did you follow through anyway?

Think of someone who always complains about not having "strategic" or "challenging" work. What could this person do differently to impress leadership and get better assignments?

Do you have any responsibilities now where you feel you worked to earn trust and then were awarded the opportunity to do more important tasks? What specific actions did you take to build that trust?

7 | SUPER SHIELD

I got the job! I was going to be responsible for a 120-person call center comprised of 10 managers and 110 customer service reps. I loved the idea of having a big team of people to talk to, inspire and motivate to success. I had been tapped on the shoulder by my senior leadership to take this "opportunity assignment." When they offered me the job, I was told that I would be a great fit because they needed someone, like me, who was very experienced in call centers.

What they didn't tell me was they needed someone naïve enough to take this job without asking about the current performance. Turns out this call center's results had been last in the state for five years straight. As I assessed my new team, I realized we had a very sick animal. The union and the managers were practically at war, and only about 50% of the work force showed up each day. So I rolled up my sleeves, busted out the incentive dollars and started running sales contests to motivate my team and bring in some fresh energy.

At first, with all the fire in my belly, I saw a nice lift in performance. Results, attendance and morale all improved. But shortly thereafter, progress slowed, and the bright, shiny enthusiasm started to wear off.

During this process, my boss kept asking me if I had the right management team to make the big changes I was pursuing. "Of course," I kept saying. I thought that was my job. I wanted to shield my new team from upper management. I would have my managers' backs and they would have mine. That is how it works, right? But here is the truth: I never held my management team accountable for their abysmal performance. They started to learn that they could produce "reasons" for their horrid results (I would later rename these "excuses").

Where I went wrong: I expected to change the entire culture solo. I never considered the fact that this group of managers had a 5-year history of poor performance. I should have considered that my management team might require a shake-up, because they were part of the problem by reverting to their old behaviors and poor performing ways.

I now see how many of them were smiling and nodding in meetings, and then doing their own thing behind my back. They knew, despite all my words, hand waiving and fist pounding, that I wasn't going to be an enforcer. I should have made sure they understood that poor performance had consequences. Instead, I was protecting them from the company and my boss, but not from themselves. I later learned that after I left this call center, it was closed. I regret not having taken the rights steps. I should have held everyone accountable and replaced the managers who weren't up to the task of helping me turn everything around. Maybe if I had done that, the call center would still be open.

LESSON LEARNED

Everyone likes success, but no one likes to be held accountable for poor performance. Fewer still like the actual act of performance management.

The challenge is, you build a strong bond with a team of leaders, and then all of a sudden there is a chink in the armor. One of your chickens stops producing eggs.

At first you go through the steps of motivation,
"Hey, you can turn it around."

Then you go through the asking stage,
"What can I do to help you?"

Next, you graduate to,
"Hey, I really need you to step it up."

And if performance is still lacking, you may find yourself at the,
"I am putting you on a performance plan so we can structure the coaching you need to be successful," stage.

Yes, this is difficult. But it's critical if you are going to be a successful leader. In fact, handling the accountability part of leadership is one of the most important skills to develop if you really care about your people being successful. Many of them need you to take this step. Be brave enough to do it.

Later in my career, I learned that instead of firing people, performance management often turned an employee around. I don't have a formal stat, but I would bet 90% of the people I have supported through performance plans were eventually successful in their roles. In fact, many later thanked me for putting them on plans. They said things like, "I had lost my motivation," or, "I just got lazy and this woke me up." I even had one manager in my organization go from not getting a raise, not getting a commission check and almost losing her job, to becoming the #1 performer in her center. She credits her turnaround to being put on a formal performance plan. Go figure!

But it doesn't work all the time. For those who are not a good fit for the job, recognition of poor results can move you down the path to termination. Sometimes this is inevitable. Occasionally, after a direct conversation, employees may self-select to leave. They realize they are miserable being in a job where they perform poorly, and it is not a fit.

The bottom line is this, if you make room for mediocre employees, then you will get mediocre results. It is that simple. For those of you who think this is harsh, think of the worst boss you have ever had and the anger you felt towards the person who kept them over you. "Why haven't they removed this awful leader yet?" you would cry at happy hour. Well, when you are in charge, it is your turn to take the right steps.

Coaching to success is the goal; but sometimes you need to coach people out the door. It is truly the best way to protect your success, and most importantly, protect your entire team.

Reagan's RULE

Protecting your people does not always protect them. Hold people accountable for their performance.

PUTTING IT TO WORK

Have you ever received brutally honest feedback that hurt at first, but you later realized was totally true? How did you feel about the person who gave you the information?

Is there an employee in your work place who isn't pulling his weight or performing as he is should? What is he specifically doing or not doing?

What actions could you take to get him to step it up? Are you doing anything to enable this poor performance?

A A+
Attitude

P People
Person

P Proactive
Stance

L Long Term
View

E Every
Mistake
Matters

PROACTIVE STANCE

Don't sit on the sidelines.
More often than not, you determine
your own opportunities.

8 | WHAT TRAINING?

I was offered my first Chief of Staff position the day before Thanksgiving. In fact, the staffing manager called me at 4 p.m. on Wednesday. I missed her call, so the holiday weekend was a long one – four days contemplating my offer and relocation package. My brain was on fire!

First thing Monday, I was on the phone with HR, getting my list of questions answered. I accepted the offer and moved to Dallas in a mere two weeks! That is the life of a Chief of Staff – move quickly, keep up, GO GO GO!

Once in Dallas, I reported to Joyce Renner, Senior Vice President. Within the first 30 days I had to:

- Learn all about a different division of the business, knowing a total of zero people in this department.

- Establish new sales and performance targets for 20,000+ people in the organization, based on the new direction of my leader.

- Discover all of my new boss's preferences, quirks and eccentricities.

- Plan a kick-off event for 40+ general managers in less than 2 weeks.

- Figure out how to merge from I-635 to I-35, without getting killed by trucks with "Texan and Proud" bumper stickers.

I received no training. Seriously, I learned by begging. I begged every single person I could to teach me something. I found former Chiefs of Staff and asked them questions about what I should be doing every day. I called my boss's old support person for tips and tricks, so I didn't accidentally step on a land mine. I called current support personnel to learn what font to use for my PowerPoint slides. Fortunately, I learned in the nick of time that using Times New Roman instead of Calibri could've been fatal. Hallelujah!

What I mostly did was jump in and start setting up conference calls, returning e-mails, and building PowerPoint presentations, without a single clue what I was doing. I never stopped to even breathe in those first few weeks. I learned the hard way that there was no manual for my job and obviously no highway patrol to monitor those trucks. Time to roll up my sleeves and lay on the horn.

LESSON LEARNED

I always laugh when people say, "I never received training when I started my job." Yeah...welcome to the club. The thing about corporate America is that a position does not just "get created" because there is a need. Someone, who is totally overwhelmed in his current role, has to whittle out enough time to make a business case justifying a new hire and promise the company his second-born child. So, by the time you come bebopping into your newly created position, your boss's hair is on fire and singeing through to his scalp.

You might think it is easier to step into a job that was recently vacated; don't hold your breath. The person who was previously in your role is usually long gone and drinking from his or her own fire hose by the time you are ready for your "transition meetings." If you think anyone has time to just sit and train you, you are living in a fantasy. It doesn't make it right, but it is what it is.

You have to get really good at hunting and begging. My approach was to look people up on the internal org chart and send an instant message, begging for a couple of minutes. I asked a few questions, and then exited quickly before I wore out my welcome. I wrote everything down and pieced it all together later.

That said, my biggest lesson with this cross-country extravaganza was: the fastest way to learn a job is to do the job. I know that sounds a little crazy because how are you supposed to do something you don't know how to do? You have to trust yourself. You were hired because someone believed in you. When you jump in with an oar and start rowing, you see connections faster and you gain confidence! Like Nike...Just DO IT.

But consider yourself WARNED: you will make mistakes. Get over it! Learn quickly, apologize, and keep going. People are forgiving of someone who says, "Man, I am so sorry. I thought I was helping." What you don't want to do is be the newbie who messes up and says, "Well don't blame me. My boss never trained me on that."

So get in that car, start the engine, accelerate and merge onto I-35. Pretty soon those trucks will be afraid of you.

Reagan's RULE

Stop waiting to be trained. Go find creative ways to train yourself.

PUTTING IT TO WORK

Consider your current position. How comprehensive was your training when you started?

If people started in your role right now, who would you advise they meet with in order to learn the job faster? (Note: if you start a new role, ask your new peers this question.)

What important skill did you learn by just doing, even if it meant you had a few stumbles as first?

CHAPTER
9

**CONTRIBUTE
ANY WAY
YOU CAN**

I had no idea what Alex Simpson was talking about, but I was a brand new Marketing Manager and he was a Vice President. He was angry, several levels above me and for some insane reason, he thought I had influence. Who was I to correct him?

Alex had a problem. He was signing programming deals with major TV networks, and they happened to make a living on commercial advertising revenue. Our new cable television service needed all these popular channels to make our service a success. However, our remote had a skip button that allowed you to breeze right through commercials. This, of course, was a fan favorite for customers, but not for people who sell advertising for a living.

Since product marketing owned the remote design, and I was in marketing, Alex came to me. I nodded a lot and said things like, "Yeah, I totally understand how that won't work." Then, eventually, I had the presence of mind to say, "Let me make a call and get something going on this."

I furiously dialed my boss and filled him in. I literally repeated word for word what I had been told. My boss understood the problem and got moving on a resolution right away. I reported back to Alex that marketing was "working on it," and we would update him as soon as possible. From that day forward, the Vice Presidents in the office came to me to resolve various marketing issues, and I always did what I could to help. It was a great way for me to build trust with a very experienced team of leaders. I am sure they had no idea what my actual job was, but then again, I was so new, neither did I.

LESSON LEARNED

Have you ever heard the saying, "Trust is not given, it's earned." There is a lot of truth to that statement in the workplace. When you are a rookie, you cannot expect that others will trust you and willingly give you the most interesting and challenging projects. The best projects are usually the ones with the most exposure, most cost, and most risk. Those assignments are earned, and in fact, they are earned on the backs of a thousand little jobs done right.

I have often heard bright young MBA grads express disdain for the "busy work" they are assigned. I also hear them say things like, "This is a waste of my time," and my favorite, "I wasn't hired for this." Even professional athletes have busy work. Shannon Sharpe, Hall of Fame tight end, once said, "You pay me to work out, I play the games for free."

No one is exempt from the grind, but not everyone is good at using it as a differentiator. I learned that the fastest way to gain trust when I start a job is roll up my sleeves, grab a shovel and start digging. Use the busy work to your advantage. If you are the only one willing to do it, you become an instant hero. If you are asked to help, don't whine, don't complain, just find a way to add value, even if it requires doing small and trivial tasks. The truth is, the person who is giving you the task doesn't see it as "mundane." It is an important piece of a larger puzzle, and when you treat it as such, you earn trust. Eventually, you push for more responsibility, and you will have the credibility and track record to be awarded it. Stay the course and you will get more challenging roles that are more rewarding and better aligned with your career goals. Eventually, you have a job you are proud of and everyone knows exactly what you do.

Reagan's RULE

Don't wait to contribute in a new job. If you see a way to help, jump in and do it.

PUTTING IT TO WORK

Think back to your first days on the job.

What seemingly trivial tasks were you assigned?

What did you learn by doing them?

Who took note of your willingness to pick up that shovel?

What mundane task could you do today that might get you noticed and lead to better assignments?

CHAPTER	**FIND THE**
10	**SMARTEST PERSON IN THE ROOM**

I was 21 years old, ambitious and totally motivated. It was my first job out of college. I was like a freight train barreling down the tracks, loaded up on Pixy Stix and caffeine. I was a brand new manager in my call center with 17 bright shiny service reps who were hoping I would be their next great boss. Ryan Sheridan, on the other hand, was the smooth operator who dominated the top of our manager scorecard in my call center. I was in awe. He was so calm and collected. He knew when to have fun, he knew when to get serious, and he knew when to give his folks a look that meant business. I bounded up to his cube daily and tried my best to copy everything he did since he was so successful in our role. I honestly think he thought I was nuts (or a stalker), but he could see one thing... I had passion.

Without a doubt, my energy and enthusiasm kept him interested. He worked with me and worked with me, and like a camel in the desert, I lapped it all up. The more I copied and made his strategies my own, the more success I had. Pretty soon, it was a neck and neck battle at the top of the scorecard with each of us switching off as lead dog. Of course I gave him all the credit, and happily, we became close friends. When I left that office for my next rotation in the company, we had a very touching big brother - little sister moment that I'll never forget. I was his protégé, and he could not have been more proud to transform me, an insane squirrel, into a leader.

LESSON LEARNED

When you're new on the job, one major problem is that you don't have any experience. It's one of those pesky things that can get in the way of your having great success and avoiding really dumb mistakes. But since you can't Google "experience," and somehow gain it, or buy it on Amazon Prime and get it in two days, you have to find a way around this problem.

My strategy is to find the smartest, most successful person in my new office and emulate his or her every move. I make a plan to soak up every single thing this successful leader does and is willing to share with me. Now you might ask, "Reagan, what if that person doesn't want to be my friend?" There is an off chance this will happen. But here is the truth about successful people: they are leaders. They like projects. They tend to be the types who want to help others and find fulfillment in seeing new projects blossom. You need to let these people know that you are a blank canvas, ready and willing to take guidance and be that new project. So, how do you do this?

There are some important keys to making successful people notice you and be willing to mentor you. First, you have to listen. That means shelve your own ideas and take in everything they say. Write it all down because it is super-annoying to have to repeat. Ask thoughtful questions.

Remember, these are the busiest people you work with, so don't be a nuisance. Even if you don't have a clue what they are talking about, write it down anyway. Even if you disagree with what they are saying, write it down. Take it all in. Lap up every drop of advice they are willing to give. You can sort it all out later, on your own.

Second, you actually have to implement some of what you learned. Nothing is more irritating than meeting with someone, taking this person's valuable time and implementing a grand total of nothing. It is insulting. You need to demonstrate that you learned something by taking action. So, don't be that annoying person. If you take up a high performer's time, implement something! Even if you do it poorly at first, your effort will be appreciated.

The younger you are and the newer you are in your role, the more likely you should just straight out copy what you see and hear. Don't have an ego about it. If I had a dollar for every time I've heard a sentence like this, "Well, when I was getting my Harvard MBA, we did a case study on ABC, and this is what study group said we should do," I'd be crazy rich. I realize you think your education makes you an expert, and it certainly does help. But the successful person in front of you is not in a book as a hypothetical situation. This person is experienced, proven, and is showing you the ropes. For real. So, try what is suggested first, and then eventually you can tweak and add your own spin.

As you get further along in your career and gain more experience, you can then start morphing their successes into your own personal strategy. Before you know it, 10 years flash by, and a young pup will come to your office, asking you for advice.

Find the most successful person in your office. Ask this leader to mentor you, and then implement the advice.

PUTTING IT TO WORK

Who is the most successful person in your work place? What do you observe he or she does that makes them so successful? What could you do to implement some of those practices?

Have you ever asked this person to mentor you and give you advice? List two topics you would discuss if you only had 15 minutes on their calendar. Now go ask for some time!

If you are already a high performer, what are you doing to mentor new employees that start in your department? You were new once as well... pay it forward!

CHAPTER

11

MAKING IT TO THE BIG LEAGUES

The lady at the door was distracted. I figured if I just looked like I belonged, she wouldn't stop me. I grabbed my folder, avoided eye contact, and walked confidently into the auditorium. Success!

I strolled around that UCLA Summer Internship Fair and tried to act like I was one of the gang. It wasn't until I started handing out resumes that reality set in. "Um, you can have this back. We are only here recruiting UCLA students." It was discouraging, but I had driven an hour and a half in LA traffic from my small school to have a chance in the big leagues.

I walked up to Pac Bell and handed the recruiter my resume. He was friendly, took a hearty scan and said, "Wait a minute. You don't go to UCLA."

Here we go again, I thought.

But he was still looking down, scanning my resume. "Very impressive," he continued. "You drove all the way down here to try for an internship. Shows a lot of initiative. Plus, you already have great work experience."

JACKPOT! I was so excited that a big company was interested in me. A casual conversation at the Internship Fair led to several rounds of interviews, which eventually led to a summer internship. Somehow my small no-name school "issue" was forgotten. Don't ask me how! I couldn't believe it! I'd landed one of the coveted spots in a summer program over a UCLA student.

Someone forgot to tell me that I was supposed to enjoy my last summer of freedom before graduation. Actually I did. But not in the European travel – beach vacay – chill kinda way. I was nose to the grindstone the entire summer. And I loved every minute of it! I was a natural fit in the corporate environment. It was great meeting people from big schools. Their education seemed so fancy to me. They attended classes that were larger than the entire student body at my small business school! Did I feel a little (more than a little!) overwhelmed by their cred? Oh yeah!

One July day, the company took us Pac Bell interns to Disneyland. It was under the guise of "team building," but really, the plan was to entice the big-school students to take a full-time job after graduation. The instructions were clear. Enjoy your day, but make sure you meet at the parking garage at 4 p.m. Got it.

I showed up on time, as instructed. But wait a minute... where were the two girls from Stanford? They were missing. We called their cell phones. We paged them (yes, this was the age of pagers). No response. Finally, after 45 minutes, and massive traffic building on the LA freeways, they emerged. They were in tears and obviously traumatized. "We got on the wrong tram and couldn't find our way," they blubbered.

It was at that exact moment that my entire mindset changed. These girls went to Stanford, and they couldn't even get on the right tram!? Maybe I have a chance at competing after all. Right then and there, I stopped apologizing. I stopped feeling inferior. I stopped feeling like because of where I came from, that ANYTHING was out of my reach.

At the end of that summer, it was this small school player who was offered that full time job. I may have snuck into the internship fair, but with my hard work, smarts and remarkable ability to locate the Disneyland parking garage, I earned my spot on the roster.

LESSON LEARNED

There are times in your career when you have to make things happen. If you want an opportunity, find a creative way to get there. Don't let an imaginary barrier stop you from going after what you want. Meet someone who knows someone who can introduce you to someone. Take initiative.

There is never a shortage of excuses on why people say they cannot get the job or the career they want.

"I don't play golf"

"I don't have the right wardrobe"

"I am from the wrong side of town"

"My kids don't go to the popular Montessori pre-school"
(OK, maybe I only heard that last one in LA.)

My point is, if you want to use an excuse you usually don't have to go far to find one.

One very popular reason I hear career doors will open and shut, surround what school someone went to. It is true that where you went to school can play a role in your opportunities, but it doesn't dictate your career. If you went to a small, or online school, it does not mean you are not every bit as smart and hard-working as your Ivy League/ big school counterpart. However, it may be harder for you to network your way into a good job. Don't let that stop you. It just means you have to be more creative.

If you went to a big school, you have a tremendous advantage, unless you choose not to use it. When there are events on campus, GO! If there is an alumni event in your area, GO! Get involved, build your network, and make sure you leverage every single resource at your disposal. If you think because you attended an academic powerhouse you will be handed jobs, you are mistaken. Even at these schools, great opportunities are competitive, and you won't get considered if you don't get in the game.

Ultimately, businesses are looking for motivated employees, regardless of where they came from (or what their golf handicap is). A school name or networking connection might get you in the door, but it is what you do with that chance that counts. Take your opportunities seriously and look fervently for open doors. If the door you want to go through isn't open, figure out how to break in. And likely it's that kind of smarts that will put you exactly where you want to be.

One of the best examples of this approach was used on me. I spoke to a group of business students at my alma mater. After my presentation, a student came bounding up to the podium. She followed up several times in the weeks following and made sure I had her resume. She wanted to be in marketing, and I was in marketing. She made sure I knew who she was and what she wanted to do. She had a focus and put in the hard work to get to her goal. Six months later, I hired her. This example involves a college student, but isn't it remarkable that she showed more motivation and fortitude than a lot of experienced employees?

It is very easy to talk yourself out of opportunities. I am not good enough. I am not fast enough. I am not experienced enough. Don't get me wrong, a healthy reality check is always good. But I find that people use these reasons as excuses not to try at all.

So, if you see a job, a career or an opportunity you want, find a way to go after it. Don't wait for an invitation to join the big leagues. Walk right onto the field and take your position.

Reagan's RULE

Don't let a perceived barrier stop you from going after an opportunity you really want.

PUTTING IT TO WORK

Has there ever been a job you wanted, but you let an "excuse" discourage you from going after it?

Describe a time that you were slightly intimidated by those around you. How did you step it up and impress your peers?

Is there a network or connection you are not leveraging? How can you foster that connection before you need it?

CHAPTER 12

YOU ARE CORDIALLY INVITED TO TAKE A RISK... NO RSVP REQUIRED

My team was not even close to making its sales goal. I was a first-time sales manager and a first-time failure in the making. So, when I heard that we could earn triple sales credit for large data connections sold to corporations, I perked up. I was never going to make my quota selling onesie-twosie landlines to a couple of small businesses. I needed something much bigger.

Here was the problem. I had no idea what a large data connection line was and neither did anyone on my team. We had never sold one...ever. I asked around...still no info. But, I didn't let that deter me. I knew this guy, Jimmy, in our technical sales support department, and he knew what a large data connection was. This began the education of Reagan, and subsequently, my team.

I met with Jimmy as often as I could. I took furious notes as he walked me through the suite of high end data products. He told me that if my team could get a legitimate lead, that he would help us close the deal. "OK," I thought, "my people don't have to be experts. They just have to be knowledgeable and confident enough to guide a business customer through the decision-making process about this product." I'm seeing triple credits in my future!

I took four large easels, and I mapped out the basics of each product. I stuck one easel on each wall of our conference room. I created training presentations and walked my team through the four products. Yes, it was a lot to learn, but my team was excited at the prospect of a big commission check. Some of my peers thought it was risky to spend a lot of sales time off the production floor, learning these new products, but I believed it was an investment worth making.

At first, I saw absolutely no leads. Then, one day, my most enthusiastic salesperson came bounding up to me, "I have a customer who is interested in a large connection!" She was bouncing off the walls!

When I finally got her settled, she explained that she'd used the training info from the east wall of the conference room and talked this potential customer through the important points. Perfect! Now the hand-off to Jimmy. He took the lead and closed the deal! Our team was ecstatic! Our large data connection translated into 102% of our sales quota and handsome commission checks for all!

LESSON LEARNED

Failure is a scary thing, and having your name squarely attached to something that is risky or out of the box can be unsettling. Risk taking isn't for everyone. But for those of us who aspire to leadership roles, career advancement and bigger paychecks, taking calculated risks is your ticket. If this is you, keep reading.

You need to own and solve a problem. You need to do something that will make you stand out from the crowd. You need to think of options, theories and possibilities because that's exactly when brilliance occurs. Innovation happens when someone thinks there could be a newer, better, smarter alternative and (here's the big piece...stay with me) takes action!

Now, let me be clear. I am not advocating reinventing the wheel for the sake of reinventing the wheel. That's stupidity. If you are new to your role, don't ignore all warnings and just do your own thing because you feel like it. Look for places to evolve the current process. Ask tons of questions so you clearly understand things that may have been overlooked. Get the history. Have a clear understanding of why things are done the way they are currently. Sometimes, what feels obvious to you with your new eyes, feels very innovative to people who have been in the role for years. Find those areas and run with them.

Understand that you might not hit a home run with these ideas, especially at first. In fact, if you are a risk taker, know you will fail. But if you keep trying and innovating, the likelihood is, you will hit a double or triple, and eventually a home run. Know this: if you don't take a risk, you never will score! I once heard an executive say, "If you are not failing, you are not really trying." It's not that he wanted his people to fail. But, he knew that if his team always took the safe path, and never took any

CHAPTER 12 | YOU ARE CORDIALLY INVITE TO TAKE A RISK...NO RSVP REQUIRED   71 risk at all, they would fall behind and miss opportunity.

Many great entrepreneurs are famous for their failures. Henry Ford, R.H. Macy, Steve Jobs and Bill Gates are just a few who come to mind. Each saw an opportunity and didn't wait on an invite. They learned from their failures and eventually had huge successes!

Reagan's RULE

Don't wait on an invitation to innovate. Advancement requires proactive risk taking.

PUTTING IT TO WORK

Describe a problem in your work place and how you think it could be solved.

How could you implement your solution?

What is the risk if you fail?

What could you achieve if you succeed?

A A+
Attitude

P People
Person

P Proactive
Stance

L **Long Term
View**

E Every
Mistake
Matters

LONG TERM VIEW

This is a marathon not a sprint.
Look out on the horizon for
career success, not just job success.

CHAPTER

13

WHERE IS THE GRASS GREENER?

I am a Californian. I am one of the rare birds who was actually born and raised in "SoCal." In fact, I lived in the same home from the time I was born until the time I graduated from college. So, when my company asked me what cities I would be willing to live in outside of LA, I listed them in order: San Diego, San Francisco and San Jose. When pressed, I very generously added to the list, Seattle and Denver. The problem is, the company headquarters is in Dallas. So, it was not extremely popular (or particularly wise) when I said things like, "I can't live in Dallas. I don't own cowboy boots. I don't like country music. And I don't wear anything Brighton or Bedazzled."

Fast forward...I got a call early one morning from my boss's boss. He explained that my name was being floated for a Chief of Staff position in our wireless division. Luckily, he was someone who gave great advice and was always straight with me. He very candidly said, "As I see it, you have two choices if you want to advance your career: move to Dallas or leave the company. This is a really good opportunity to springboard your career or a good way to kill it if you say no." Well, no sugar coating there, but I appreciated the honesty. So, like everything else we say we will never do, I actually considered a move to Dallas.

That swift kick was just what I needed. So my husband and I plugged our noses, and jumped into the deep end that is called North Texas. In LA, my career had stalled for eight years straight. Once in Dallas, I was promoted two times in a row, making General Manager and Assistant Vice President in record time. I guess the stars at night are not the only big and bright things, deep in the heart of Texas (clap, clap, clap, clap).

LESSON LEARNED

There are three types of people at my Fortune 500 company. The first are those who are specialists. They love their work. They have really complex titles that most of us don't understand, and degrees I cannot pronounce. These people are perfectly content doing their jobs for an entire career.

Then there are those who are generalists. They are up for "whatever." They will move anywhere, do anything and take on any challenge. They move up quickly in the company and earn nicknames like, "the fix it guy" or "clean up gal." They are the types who thrive on change and hold their zip codes and titles loosely.

Then there is the third type – the ones I refer to as the "inflexibles." These people do not want to move, do not want to change departments, but do want raises and promotions. In corporate America, they are typically very unhappy. They feel like they are "due" a promotion because they are top performers. The challenge is that they live in rural America or somewhere that isn't where the primary decision-makers reside. They don't want to give up their five-acre ranch for city life. Or they don't want to sell the house with the new gourmet kitchen. Or perhaps they like their department and can't quite grasp why they should have to learn something different. Why should they have to do silly things like move to headquarters for a promotion? They have no interest in learning about the company's Atlanta operations, when they are clearly the queen or king of their department in Scranton.

You might be the best performer in your department. I was. But often times what is lacking is not you or your performance. It's opportunity. And more often than not, if advancement is part of your plan, you will need to change, adapt and most likely, relocate.

Whether you consider yourself a Generalist, Specialist or an Inflexible, you should be aware of likely consequences. Expecting the corporation to bend to your will is not a good strategy. It's also highly unlikely. Somewhere along the way, you need to decide what your priorities are and what kind of worker you want to be. If you love HR, go for it, but understand that it might slow your growth to stay in one department. If you love your city but aren't in a strategic locale, understand that probably means a longer path to the top. Specialists will be energized by going deeper in knowledge about their field, instead of trying to go wide and learn about the entire business. Seek out ways that will keep you sharp in your field, if you want to have opportunities as a Specialist.

But, if you are the type who has a spouse, family, or pet and everyone is up for an adventure, your route up the corporate ladder may be faster. Are you willing to put all the chips on the table and take the crazy assignment in Shanghai? Showing your willingness for whatever will yield great rewards, but the flip side is, it can take its toll. The third time you pull your high-schooler out to move might cause a rift you cannot repair. Know yourself, know your family, and make wise choices. If you do, you may find out the grass really is greener on the other side of the world.

Reagan's RULE

Know what matters most to you. If your priority is opportunity, be open to changing roles and locations.

PUTTING IT TO WORK

Do you consider yourself a Specialist, Generalist or an Inflexible?

Have you ever been presented with an opportunity that involved a move? If so, what were the factors that aided you in making your decision?

Is there someone in your workplace who might have furthered her career, if she'd been willing to transfer to another division?

14 | FISH OUT OF WATER

I was in the second rotation of my leadership program, and it was the one that everyone dreaded. If you were a techy/engineer-type, you had to take a sales manager job. If you were a salesy/marketing-type, you had to take a technical manager job. Sigh. That meant I was sentenced to 12 months in a garage with phone technicians. You know, the hardhat wearing, pole climbing, tool belt slinging kind, that drive around in gigantic phone trucks.

Not only was I not technical, I was:

- One of 5 women in a 150–person garage

- One of 4 people under 30

- The only woman under 30...period

In other words, to say that I "stuck out like a sore thumb" was the understatement of the year. But there I was, chipper and ready each morning, dressed in my khaki pants, oversized men's polo shirt, and steel-toed work boots. That was me... jumping up and down trying to motivate my techs to be safe and efficient, like never before.

As you can imagine, this scenario produced some interesting situations. One time in particular, Terry Stephenson decided it would be a good idea to hit on me, in front of everyone on the floor. He was a middle-aged man, with leathery tan skin, who sat on his boat every weekend drinking Natty Light. He thought he was big time and wanted to prove it to everyone by testing the new, young, and totally out of her comfort zone manager. So, he casually called out, loud enough for everyone to hear, "Hey Reagan, you want to go out sometime."

After my initial shock and annoyance, I responded, "Terry, I am engaged."

His response was classic. He snorted and said even louder, "Great, that means you are still available!"

I just walked away shaking my head. If this was my "out of the box" rotation, does that mean I was allowed to throw the box at his head?

LESSON LEARNED

It can be culture shock when you have to wade into the waves of another ocean. You take an assignment in a different department and you look around your workplace, wondering if anyone even speaks your language. What do you do in this situation? You need to figure out how to navigate the waters. And you need to figure it out fast!

First of all, do not apologize for being different. It is what makes you unique, and that is great. It can be a major strength if you bring a different background, thought process and set of experiences to an entrenched work force. You can be a breath of fresh air that helps your team evolve. Do not be discouraged when you meet resistance. You should expect your team to push back, test you, resist change and find strategies to protect their turf. Your job is to find creative ways to advance your initiatives, push the limits and prioritize the battles that are really worth fighting.

At the same time, stay humble. You are not special or better because you are different. There is immense value in the tacit information that can only be gained through experience. I see time and again, college graduates coming into a blue collar environment and thinking because they have a degree hanging on a wall, they are better and smarter than hard working union employees. You are 22 years old and you are supervising someone who has 22 years of experience, think long and hard about your approach. These people have skills and expertise that is to be respected and appreciated.

As much as you might bring a fresh perspective to a new department, take advantage of the perspective this experience is giving you. It is sharpening you in ways a comfortable environment never will. When you return to a role that's in your comfort zone, I guarantee you'll look back at your out-of-the-box experience with some incredible life lessons you'll always remember.

I'd even bet that you will come to appreciate the people who are different in your wheel house. These are the people who come into your office and challenge the status quo. You might actually listen to these newcomers with an open mind. Rather than shutting out different thinking, you will remember when you were that fish out of water.

Reagan's RULE

Different is good, it just isn't easy.

PUTTING IT TO WORK

Reflect on a situation where you were the odd man (or woman) out in the workplace. How did you move from stranger to teammate?

Look around your workplace. Who is feeling out of place? How can you help this person adjust to the environment? What can you gain from their fresh perspective?

What was an unexpected lesson you learned from an older, more experienced co-worker?

THE SQUIRREL LADY

It was my first opportunity to work on an, "Executive Escalation." This was a customer who had complained so many times via phone calls, letters and e-mails, that the office of our company's president was handling their issue personally. What made these encounters particularly fun was that you got to meet with the customers face to face, in their homes, to discuss what they were stark raving mad about. The notes on the e-mail were a little fuzzy and did not seem normal, even for these extreme cases. There was something about a tree, a telephone pole and a squirrel attack. My buddy, Darren, was never one to miss a show, so he offered to come along and help me investigate.

When we showed up at the house, a woman, in a bathrobe, came scurrying out from what appeared to be a garage apartment. She looked very relieved and excited that we were there. Before we could even get out a greeting, she was thanking us for coming and telling us she would show us the problem. She pointed to a tree branch in a neighbor's yard that had grown full of leaves, and now touched the telephone wire in her backyard. "This is how they get into my yard," she explained. We waited. "The squirrels climb up the tree, cross over from that branch, walk across the wire, down your telephone pole and threaten me."

For the next 30 minutes, she proceeded to explain how this was unfair and how we needed to find a way to clear the branch away from our telephone wires. She then told us how she had written notes on a blue lined paper, made paper airplanes and threw them into the neighbor's yard – the neighbors who owned the offending tree. (Side note: We did, in fact, go to the neighbor's yard and found no less than 5 paper airplanes laying just beyond the fence.)

I had to give her credit for creativity, but I wasn't surprised when she said the neighbors had not contacted her. Darren and I did a lot of apologizing, a lot of listening, and a lot of avoiding eye contact with each other – trying to keep from busting out laughing. We had to, very gently, explain that we only cut foliage away from a telephone wire when it was in imminent danger of taking customers out of service.

It was about this time when the back door of the main house opened. An elderly woman appeared and yelled, "Jill, what are you doing out here? Are you bothering them about the squirrels? You need to let that go." After a painfully awkward exchange between Jill and her mom, we realized that this squirrel attack discourse was a regular occurrence. We backed away slowly and apologized for her obviously dire squirrel situation. We had avoided a scene and of course an attack from the squirrels...barely.

LESSON LEARNED

Customers are pretty darn important. As it turns out, you cannot actually run a business without them. They supply this very important thing called revenue. They also require something called customer service. Understanding your customers and what they need is fundamental to being a successful leader.

That said, customer service jobs are not usually sexy. Rarely do those with customer service titles work on high exposure projects. They don't get handed big fancy budgets. They don't have attractive hours. But, that does not man they are not highly important for your organization and for your career.

Frequently, young college grads are looking for assignments that are fun and glamorous – definitely not adjectives that describe positions like "call center manager, "store manager" and "installation manager." It is, however, in these jobs that you learn the most about yourself, the front line, and the customers in your business. It is the fuel you need to power you towards those HR, Marketing, Administration and Biz Dev jobs you really want.

The risk, when you get too far from the customer, is losing touch with the reality of the business. It is easy to tell which people in the staff departments have had front line experience and which ones have not. The ones who haven't are far more likely to say things like, "our store reps should just sell more of this," and, "I don't understand why this process is so hard," and, "In testing, this product was very successful." Don't be that guy. Do not be the clueless person who doesn't understand that there are live bullets on the front line. Know that the front line employees need sympathetic, humble and hardworking support teams to help them, not judge them. The best way to learn what it's really like in the trenches is to do the front line jobs yourself. Everybody needs a "squirrel lady" story of their own, to understand those who have them every day.

Reagan's RULE

Never get too far from your customer.

PUTTING IT TO WORK

Tell a customer service story. Were you the crazy customer or the customer service rep?

Have you ever been in a meeting and the person talking seems totally disconnected from the reality of the day-to-day business? How successful was this person's message?

Make a list of jobs at your workplace that touch the customer directly. Which of these positions should you pursue at some point in your career? If you are not in one of these jobs now, what 2-3 activities can you do to make sure you stay connected to the needs and experiences of the people in those roles?

CHAPTER 1

TO MBA OR NOT TO MBA: THAT IS THE QUESTION

16

I was ready for a change. I had reached a point in my career where I wanted to do something totally new. Coincidentally, I got a call from a friend, saying her marketing department was hiring. While my undergrad degree was in marketing, I had never actually worked in the field.

What to do? I jumped on the opportunity and did my best to convince the interviewer that my leadership experience would translate – from managing people to managing direct mail campaigns. As I anxiously waited to see if I would get the job, I did some research to learn more about my potential, new employer. I learned that the Vice President of Marketing over this group was a mentor of mine years ago. I couldn't believe it! I dropped Mr. Mentor a note, letting him know I was interviewing for a job in his organization. A few days went by, and I got a call from staffing – with a job offer. Booyah!

Days later, I finally got a response from Mr. Mentor. "By the time I received your email, you already had the job," he explained. "Glad you will be joining our team, but I need to make something clear to you." My stomach dropped. Oh no, this job comes with a catch. Mr. Mentor, now Mr. Vice President of my new team said, "You must enroll in an MBA program. I don't care where you go. But as someone who is invested in your career, I will not let you take this job without a promise that you will enroll as soon as possible. You will really benefit, and I know that if I don't push you now, you won't go back at all. Got it?" Boy, did I get it. I called my alma mater and discovered I could start in two weeks – in time for the spring semester.

Three years later, after taking one class each quarter, I finally graduated with my MBA. It was not easy to balance school and work, but I did it. Through the process, I understood why I had been encouraged to go back. I had taken on a highly strategic role, and my mentor knew I needed some development in that area if I was going to be successful. My MBA really sharpened my thinking, and expanded my strategic perspective. With each class I learned more, which made me want to learn more. I had been pushed by my mentor to go back, but it was the drive for self-improvement that helped me finish.

LESSON LEARNED

Every time I talk to a group of recent college graduates, the master's degree question comes up. It's usually phrased like this, "Do I need a master's degree to advance my career?"

"Well, not usually," is my response. The truth is, unless you are in a specialized profession, like a doctor, lawyer or teacher, you probably don't "need" an advanced degree. What propels a career is great performance and a strong network, not another diploma hanging on your wall.

I challenge people to ask themselves if and why they "want" a master's. Whether you take a break from your full time job to go back, or you try and pull double duty, advancing your education is a sacrifice. So, instead of thinking where this degree can get you in your career, think about what it can give to you personally. How can it grow you? How can it sharpen you? What can it teach you about yourself and your industry?

In my situation, I had been working five years when I went back for a graduate degree. I will never forget the overwhelming feeling of writing my first paper for grad school. The part of my brain that knew how to properly footnote a source had atrophied. However, having work experience before getting my MBA gave me context, making the experience incredibly fulfilling.

Even though I was tired from working and commuting when I arrived for class, I was able to engage in great discussions with my peers – like-minded students who were as passionate about business as I was. And to add one more layer of icing to my sleep-deprived cake, I was able to take what I learned Tuesday night and apply it at work on Wednesday morning.

Intellectual reasons will be enough to get you started, but passion to invest in yourself will help you finish. No matter what you decide, make sure you ask the right questions. It is not *if* you should get an MBA but *why* you want one in the first place.

Continue your education for the right reason – yourself!

PUTTING IT TO WORK

List the pros and cons of continuing your education.

From an emotional standpoint, how do you feel about the prospect of returning to school? Do your friends and family think it would be a good idea?

Look around your workplace. Who has a graduate degree? Has it helped them achieve their goals?

CHAPTER 17

HEY INFLUENCER, LOOK OVER HERE!

Have you ever heard the expression, "if you want something done, find the busiest person in the room?" Yeah, that was me in my marketing job. I was working for an exploding entertainment department, and I literally set the strategy, designed the marketing pieces, and did the creative agency invoices for my campaigns. I was in LA toiling away, and the rest of my team was at headquarters in Texas. I wasn't sure all my hard work was being noticed. (I certainly didn't have big enough hair for anyone in Texas to notice me — that was for sure.)

After almost 5 years of really impressive performance, and no impressive career opportunities, I had become a little jaded. I enjoyed my job but felt like a hamster on a wheel, jogging super-fast to nowhere. I tried to stay motivated by telling myself, "This morning my wheel will roll somewhere different." Turns out, on this particular day, I was right.

I was told that a big time executive was coming out to our "remote" market to get to know the good talent. Basically, this was a minor league scouting assignment for the exec, minus the cheap motels and sunflower seeds. So, I completed my assigned pre-work, selected good questions, and of course, picked out something fabulous to wear. I came to work expecting very little, but prepared for anything. (I was smart enough to know that not being prepared could be a career killer).

This executive had a "Devil Wears Prada-esque" reputation for being tough and demanding. The conversation ended up being a hit. I was able to add some great points to the discussion and engage him with good questions. I even got him laughing! I wrote down every single thing he said about his leadership style in the 2-hour session. Good thing I did... 2 years later he would be the one to finally promote me to General Manager. The long wait was over when the right influencer noticed me...and I didn't even have to tease my hair.

LESSON LEARNED

If you want the right people to notice you, the first step is to be the best performer on your team, every single day. So, when someone actually looks under your rock, you stand out as the best thing they see. Mediocre performers with selfish attitudes are not the bright shiny objects executives are drawn to. They are looking for people who are positive, innovative and who consistently deliver great results.

Another thing you have to manage before you even step foot in front of an influential leader is your brand. A lot of high performers fall into the trap that, "my performance should speak for itself." Performance is a fantastic way to get on the radar. However, to fly above the radar you need to manage your image. Are you someone who has a good reputation?

Are you viewed as ethical and trustworthy? Do you look sharp and put together or like someone fished your pants out of the laundry basket this morning? Does your language sound professional or is it a parade of F-bombs and grammar mishaps? How about that social media account? Are you posting pictures with your niece at her 3rd birthday party, or are you posting pictures from the wild party you hit up in Cabo? Everything you put out there shapes your reputation and directly impacts your organization's willingness to invest in your career and promote you. I can't tell you how many people I know who have been passed over for opportunities because they are not managing their brand.

When you do get a chance to meet with someone in a position of influence, make sure you are prepared. By prepared, I mean you have done enough research to ask great questions. Here is why great questions matter so much. Not only do they demonstrate how smart you are, but they allow the influencers to demonstrate how smart they are. I once interviewed for a job in college and said, "Well, I don't think that went well because the interviewer did all the talking." I got the job and was then educated that people like nothing better than to hear themselves talk. This is especially true if what they are talking about is something they are passionate about. Your job is to find out what it is these big dogs care about and ask them a bunch of questions about it. You never know... those answers might come in handy years later when that person offers you a job.

Not everyone, just the right influencers need to notice you. Manage your performance and brand so you are ready to be noticed.

PUTTING IT TO WORK

Who are the influencers in your workplace?

What is important to them?

Is there anything you should be doing now, before you meet with them, to improve your performance or image?

A A+
Attitude

P People
Person

P Proactive
Stance

L Long Term
View

E Every
Mistake
Matters

EVERY MISTAKE MATTERS

Mistakes are costly. Cash in on what they can teach you each and every time.

CHAPTER **18** | **PLACING YOUR BETS**

No one believed me. I kept swearing that Doug was the best service rep on my team. I was a new manager in the call center, so all the other managers knew Doug and had managed him in the past. When I made the declaration, in a staff meeting, that Doug was my best employee, the first in line in the skeptic column was my Sales Manager. He was not buying what I was selling. I kept saying, "Doug is a great seller, customers love him, and every time I ask him to do something for the team, he is happy to help."

This all came to a head when we were trying to decide who would be my back up while I was on vacation. This was a big deal. This rep would be taken off the phones for a week and instead, lead the team. It was important because the manager played a key role in the daily operations and for the rep who was chosen, it was an opportunity that often led to even more opportunities.

As always in an office environment, a heated debate drew a crowd amongst the managers. I was standing by my man. I was placing my bets. I was insisting that Doug, despite any behaviors he had displayed in the past, was ready for more responsibility. Based on the bets from my fellow managers, my odds didn't look good. But my Sales manager, always one to listen, came up with a creative solution. He said, "Let's listen to Doug's next call. If he does a good job, I will let you give him this opportunity."

So we dialed in, put the call on speaker, and waited. Hmm. That's strange. There were customers waiting in the queue, so why wasn't Doug dialed in? Maybe he just had to finish noting an account. More waiting. And then, as if in slow motion, Doug walked by, with his jacket on and a cigarette hanging from his mouth. He had his head down as he walked out of the building for an unauthorized smoke break – in the one moment he was going to prove me right. Dealer takes all.

LESSON LEARNED

When you're young and new, you don't have baggage. That is a good thing because you bring a fresh perspective. And yes, there are times when someone has been unfairly pegged, and you will uncover an unrecognized treasure, making you a hero and your treasure forever grateful. But when you're young and inexperienced, you have no idea what is really going on. So before you jump on your high horse, scan the room. If you're the newbie, think twice before going to battle with the oldies, especially when all the oldies agree.

Also, if you're new in any role, particularly if it involves managing people, know that you're a prime target. It is very easy for people to try and manipulate you. They take advantage of the fact that you are trying to be "open" and "attentive" and "fair." They snuggle up to you and try to make you their bestie, all the while, feasting on your naiveté.

I wish I had a magic decoder ring to help you tell the difference. Over time, your ability to sniff out B.S. should grow stronger and eventually rival that of my beagle. In the meantime, I encourage you to listen carefully to what people say, but pay even closer attention to their actions. Be very slow to judge, and simply observe.

Sometimes these observations take time. There are stories of mediocre employees springing to life under the right boss. You get to be the magician who magically unlocks their true potential. But there are more stories of people faking good performance for a while to get on the new boss's good side, just to return to their lazy, low performing ways.

Listen carefully to people, particularly those who have more experience than you and those who you feel are smart and savvy. Listen for clues that can tell you if you have a diamond in the rough or a total dud. Be smart about where you place your bets, and on whom you place them.

You will bet on people and be disappointed, but don't stop believing in people all together. Just be smarter about who you bet on next time.

PUTTING IT TO WORK

Give an example of someone (friend, colleague or employee) you went to bat for and then later regretted your action. What did you learn?

Think about a time someone believed in you and it made a difference in your life. What actions did you take to earn that belief?

Name three people who you think have great "B.S." decoders. They can sniff out the truth and determine someone's true character. How do you use these people today to help you filter? How can you use their skills in the future?

CHAPTER

19

ONE
NOTE
NELLY

Perma-smile. That was me. I was always smiling.

Situation: Ted wasn't making his numbers.
My Response: "Well, I'm sure you will next month!"

Situation: Shannon wasn't coming to work tomorrow for the tenth day in a row.
My Response: "Well, I sure hope you feel better soon!"

Situation: Rafael hit my car in the parking lot.
My Response: "Oh no, are you OK??"

Our jobs on the front line were tough, and I thought I could bring some sunshine. So that was my management strategy — all sunshine, all the time. Some of my employees loved it. They thrived on being trusted and loved on. Others were sure I was abusing illegal substances. Then there were the ones who, for some reason, didn't respond to me at all. In fact, they seemed to be smiling at my face and doing exactly the opposite of what I was asking behind my back. Hmmm...strange.

One day my director came to my office for a visit. She was a smart and talented leader, and I really wanted to impress her.

After a couple of days observing me with my team, she said, "You can't just be one note, Reagan. Not everything is positive. You have to show a few other emotions. Make people a little nervous."

What?! I thought being a leader meant seeing the silver lining in even the worst hurricane cloud....right? It wasn't until years later that I understood this was one of the most powerful coaching moments in my career. It challenged me to overhaul my leadership philosophy, and mix in some new responses. I learned that being a one-trick pony was not the way to win the rodeo.

LESSON LEARNED

Life is a smörgåsbord of emotions. Having one note, whether negative or positive, makes you a one-dimensional leader in a multi-dimensional world. There is a time and a place in business for smiling and a time and place for a stern word. My experience is that employees need all kinds of motivation. Today, they may need an encouraging word to pump them up. Tomorrow, they might need you to challenge them and raise the bar. Occasionally, they need to be told they will be unemployed unless they improve. People are all different and require different interactions.

There are days you need to come to work and laugh with your peers. (Memo to Mr. Serious, fun is actually OK in the work place.) There are also days when you are going to wonder if the surveillance cameras are on in the parking lot, because you want to key your co-workers car. Frustration is also OK in the workplace, as long as it is channeled into constructive and clear communication (and doesn't result in handcuffs and felony charges). The trick is to respond appropriately to each situation. Some days are rosy and some are gray. Some coworkers are brilliant and smart, while others are evil lunatics. Learning to have good judgment and respond to each situation and person appropriately, will help you excel as a leader.

In my case, I started mixing in many flavors of responses into my management ice cream bowl. I now analyze situations and respond with clear and honest direction, even if it is unpopular. What I never do is behave disrespectfully. Do not mistake being firm with being rude. Public humiliation does not gain trust. It doesn't improve performance. And it's unprofessional.

Someone recently said about my style, "Reagan is a lot of fun, but you better have your 'stuff' together when you meet with her (edited version)." Sounds like someone who has a few more notes in her repertoire.

Reagan's RULE

Don't be a one-dimensional leader in a multi-dimensional world.

PUTTING IT TO WORK

Describe a manager who you consider successful?

Give an example of how this person handled a positive situation and how this manager handled a negative situation?

Is there a place where you have become a One Note Nelly and are not being successful? Could you benefit from responding differently to the situation or person?

CHAPTER **LOOSE**

20 | **LIPS SINK CAREERS**

I had just started my third rotational assignment as an Account Manager. I was selling big telephone services to big businesses. That, of course, meant I was moved into the high rise building in downtown LA. I was wearing power suits and commuting. It all sounded so cool and exactly like what I'd imagined a big, corporate job would be. So, when my mentor, a very senior ranking VP, pulled me aside to warn me about the guy sitting next to me, I was blown away. "Don't hang out with Ted. He has a reputation for flirting with young girls, and you don't want to get the rep of being one of his girls."

I was grossed out. My bubble burst. This wasn't the shiny, fantastical, ultra-professional picture I'd painted of my corporate dream job! I looked over and yes, Ted was the epitome of mid-life crisis in a box...quaffed hair, dirty mustache, shiny polyester. I'm sure he drove a red Corvette.

Having been raised a Girl Scout, I thought for sure it was my duty to help my friend, Jackie. She was hanging around with Ted! Obviously she couldn't know his true character. So, I told her what my mentor said and even quoted him, so she would know how serious this was. She nodded, mouth open, "Wow, thank you."

A couple of hours later, I was sitting in my cube, clacking away on my keyboard, when Ted came storming out of his office. He made a beeline for my cube and said, "I know what you've been saying about me and what your mentor said. If you two have a problem with me, you can say it to my face." I was speechless. Ted marched off and, let's just say, we didn't talk after that. Guess I figured out the hard way that my friend Jackie was one of Ted's girls after all.

LESSON LEARNED

Sometimes it's tricky to figure out who to trust. If you work with someone, 50+ hours a week, side-by-side, in identical cubicles, you probably think you know this person inside and out. Be careful! When you are given a piece of information that is confidential, controversial or political, it is imperative that you either keep your mouth shut or really trust the info to the right people.

Truth be told, it's tough to keep your mouth closed every time you hear or experience something – especially if it's juicy! As an extrovert, I'm the type to process information out loud, with someone. But as I move up the corporate ladder, I find it is more and more important to use discretion. As your career starts to take shape, bosses start to let you in behind the curtain, and you will see and hear things that impact your organization.

You might hear an office is closing and co-workers are going to be out of work. Or, perhaps you hear an organizational move is coming and you know a work friend is going to end up under a bad boss. It is tempting to jump in and want to help. But when that "trusted" friend tells her friends, the next thing you know, the very private piece of information you have becomes very public. As tough as it is to learn to trust your leadership, do it anyway. Have the humility to acknowledge that your bosses may actually know what they're doing. This will allow you to keep your mouth shut in some instances and keep your backside out of a lot of trouble.

Learn to become a vault. Be the kind of person a boss, mentor or friend can trust with information. If you gain a reputation for having loose lips, it can damage your friendships and your relationships with co-workers. It can also damage your career, permanently.

*Get the rep as someone who can
always be trusted with critical info.*

**PUTTING
IT TO
WORK**

Did you ever blab something and then regret it?

Has something someone said about you or your
projects, ever made its way back to your ears?
How did you feel about the situation?

Do you know something now that you'd like
to share but have used your better judgment
and opted to keep to yourself? What would the
repercussions be if this info got out?

CHAPTER

21

HEY, WHEN ABOUT ME?

I had taken a big leap of faith. I'd moved to headquarters in Dallas. I was working for a highly influential leader and was her "right hand man" as Chief of Staff. This is after I'd taken up residence on the high potential leader list for over 7 years. Yes, 7 years, at the same level, on the same list – certainly not the rapid ascent up the corporate ladder that I'd expected. It had been a very long road to promotion, but now it was about to pay big dividends.

My boss approached me about a Director of Training role. "This is perfect," I thought. I know the organization like the back of my hand. I had served in front-line roles in call centers, so I knew what this job entailed. I also had a passion for teaching and training and could pour myself into the job. I got through the first interview. I got past the second interview. Now all I had left was one last interview with a high-ranking official. I knew that meant it was down to the final two!

After the interview, I waited and waited to hear. My 10-year career was culminating in a single phone call. No pressure. The wait felt like forever, but was maybe three days. Finally, the phone call came! It was an invitation to go back and meet with interviewer number two that very afternoon. I ran up to his office with a pep in my step and a smile on my face. Then...I sat quietly as he told me I did not get the job.

He told me that he had been super impressed by me. He knew I was a talented leader and that I would be promoted soon. He shared some of his own story and how he had waited a long time to be promoted – like I had. He shared some advice that had been given to him. He said, "Reagan, if you continue to perform at the next level, eventually the title will come." My devastation was only partially soothed, but I appreciated the fact that he took the time to encourage me. I left his office, turned that devastation into motivation, and doubled my efforts to be promoted. In less than 3 months, I found myself with the title I had been working so hard to achieve.

LESSON LEARNED

Disappointment is part of the gig. You will find yourself in positions of frustration and disappointment as you try and scale the corporate ladder. It may come in the form of being passed over for an opportunity you desperately want. It might come in the form of some really tough feedback about a fatal flaw in your leadership style. It might even come in the form of being told, "You are not ready," and you have to take a lateral assignment before anyone will even consider you for a promotion.

I am not going to tell you to, "suck it up," and get over disappointment; I am going to tell you to use it. Let it be the fuel you need to improve. Take your lumps, and tell the world you are going to fight back. Listen to what is being told to you, and decide that you are going to scale the wall in front of you. Find leaders and mentors who can help you overcome your particular challenge. It might take drastic measures to move up, but if you're truly driven, you'll be willing to make those sacrifices. Then, when the job calls for someone who can be counted on – someone who can demonstrate self-improvement, it will finally be your turn.

Reagan's RULE

You will face disappointment. How you handle it will determine your career.

PUTTING IT TO WORK

Have you ever been passed over for a job you desperately wanted?

What feedback were you given, and how did you handle the disappointment?

Do you feel you're qualified to fill that role today? If so, based on what? If not, what would be required to get you there?

A A+
Attitude

P People
Person

P Proactive
Stance

L Long Term
View

E Every
Mistake
Matters

CLOSING
THOUGHTS

I have almost an obsessive need to summarize things – probably a side effect of my Type A personality. So, please indulge me while I attempt to tie up the last 21 chapters into something you can take with you on your way out the door, to help you with your career.

This book is organized into 5 main sections:

A A+ Attitude

P People Person

P Proactive stance

L Long term view

E Every mistake matters

I give you this little mnemonic to help you remember the key lessons because if you are anything like me, you will be super fired up about what you are reading now, and promptly forget it in 6 months. You will remember the squirrel lady and the boss with the cute purse (which you really should, because it was an incredible handbag...trust me), but you won't remember the key lessons that will shape your career.

So, when do you pull this bad boy out and use it? When you find your career is sidelined, and you don't know why. Look hard at the A.P.P.L.E. and figure out where you are struggling. Then take a big bite.

A+ ATTITUDE

Are you in a funk? Do you find that you are the negative person in the office who is constantly complaining? Have you reached the, "why even try, it doesn't matter" stage? Then go back to the story in the attitude section and reread it to get your attitude in order. If you don't get that straight, the rest of the book really doesn't matter. You have to have an attitude that is leaning forward, ready to go, head in the game and prepped to take life by the horns. Your attitude is a choice...daily!

PEOPLE PERSON

Once you know your attitude is in order, I find the fastest way to slow down a career is to fall down on the people part. It might be that your employees love you, but your boss has no idea what you have accomplished. It might be that your boss loves you, and your employees cannot stand your brown nosing ways. Even trickier, it could be a peer that is causing you problems. You are in la-la land doing your work, and your "colleague" is secretly plotting a way to get your parking spot. Your peers have a lot more influence than you realize. They can be a huge resource for you, or a huge pain. Use some of the lessons on observation and trust to make sure you have a healthy view of how to interact. Evaluate your relationships and revisit the stories about bosses, peers and direct reports.

PROACTIVE STANCE

Now the people part will always be a work in progress, because people are moving targets. But let's say you feel you have good relationships with above, below and beside. The next place to look is opportunity. It is sometimes knocking and we have the TV turned up so loud that we can't hear it. We have so much day-to-day, head's down focus that we miss looking around for the right, next step. Or maybe it comes knocking and we have developed a pesky habit of turning off all the lights and pretending we are not home. Being open to new experiences and opportunities is critical. There is risk with jumping in. However, you will not advance without inviting opportunity in for dinner. Revisit some of the adventures I had as I embraced opportunities. Let them inspire you to make decisions on how you want to respond when opportunity comes knocking.

LONG TERM VIEW

Maybe you feel that you take advantage of opportunities that are presented to you, but these so-called "opportunities" are always dead ends. You are super-pumped up to make a move, take a new job or work in a new industry, only to find yourself disappointed and frustrated AGAIN! This may be an indication that you have too short a view of your career. Opportunities are not an end – they are a means to an end. They are the paving stones on your path to success.

When we were kids, we experienced "devastation" because we didn't like our fourth grade teacher. Or we weren't allowed to go bowling. Life. Is. Over! Looking back it all seems silly and trivial. Fourth grade is 9 months and then you move on. New grade. New teacher. New annoying boy that sits next to you and doesn't shower. You have grades you like and grades you don't. But the goal is graduation. You survive each grade, but you never lose track of the diploma.

Somehow, in the course of our careers, we take jobs, and like our fourth grade experiences, instead of hanging in until we can move to the next grade, we decide to drop out of school. Sometimes careers require planning, risk taking and strategically changing direction. Other times the best approach is staying put. You have to think of jobs you want and then go get the building blocks of experience and education you need to get there. If you want a job, you may not be able to jump straight into it. Don't let that discourage you; let it motivate you. Line up the things you need to get where you want and then shoot them down one by one!

If you need some encouragement, peruse the sections where I had to take the long term view. My patience and persistence paid off in a big way.

EVERY MISTAKE MATTERS

Sometimes people are patient enough to build a map to success, but with the first ditch they hit, they get really discouraged. Look, mistakes are part of this journey. They are totally ugly, don't get me wrong. But they are beautiful tutors. They teach you more about leadership and success than success alone does. Failure can be devastating. But if you let it devastate you, then you have failed. If you get up, learn from the mistake, and don't make it again, you become stronger and smarter.

If you think you are immune to mistakes, then you are mistaken. I am a recovering perfectionist. I used to make it my life goal to never make mistakes. The challenge with us perfectionist types is we only give two grades – "A"s or "F"s. There is no in-between grade. But what people like my husband have taught me is that life is about the journey. It is about the mess. It is about the experiences. If all we worry about is the results, we miss the process. Don't miss the process. Let these pesky speed bumps teach you how to be a better person and leader.

If you find yourself in the midst of a mistake-fest, then go back and be encouraged by my blunders. Read how they taught me, tutored me and made me who I am today. A gal who wrote a book that someone actually bought and read all the way to the end.

Reagan's
RULE

SUMMARY OF REAGAN'S RULES

A+ ATTITUDE

THE BIG A

The right attitude is key to your success.

PEOPLE PERSON

YOUR BOSS:

DON'T JUDGE A BOSS BY HER HANDBAG

Don't be quick to write off a boss based on your first impressions. Adjust your style to meet theirs so you can work with and learn from any kind of supervisor.

YOUR PEERS:

ADULTS ARE NOT THAT DIFFERENT FROM KIDS

The office is not your personal fan club. Observe actions over time and build trust with the right people who are in your corner.

THE BOSS SAID SO

Don't name drop to get things done. Build relationships so your colleagues will want to get things done for you.

YOUR PEOPLE:

CLEAN UP ON AISLE 5

Managing humans is messy. But if done with heart, it can be the most rewarding part of your career.

THE ROPE

If you give people too much rope, too quickly, they may hang themselves with it! Release responsibility as they earn it.

SUPER SHIELD

Protecting your people does not always protect them. Hold people accountable for their performance.

PROACTIVE STANCE

WHAT TRAINING?

Stop waiting to be trained. Go find creative ways to train yourself.

CONTRIBUTE ANYWAY YOU CAN

Don't wait to contribute in a new job. If you see a way to help, jump in and do it!

FIND THE SMARTEST PERSON IN A ROOM

Find the most successful person in your office. Ask this leader to mentor you, and then implement the advice.

MAKING IT TO THE BIG LEAGUES

Don't let a perceived barrier stop you from going after an opportunity you really want.

YOU ARE CORDIALLY INVITED TO TAKE A RISK...
NO RSVP REQUIRED

Don't wait on an invitation to innovate. Advancement requires proactive risk taking.

LONG TERM VIEW

WHERE IS THE GRASS GREENER?

Know what matters most to you. If your priority is opportunity, be open to changing roles and locations.

FISH OUT OF WATER

Different is good, it just isn't easy.

THE SQUIRREL LADY

Never get too far from your customer.

TO MBA OR NOT TO MBA: THAT IS THE QUESTION

Continue your education for the right reason – yourself!

HEY INFLUENCER, LOOK OVER HERE!

Not everyone needs to notice you – just the right influencers. Manage your performance and brand so you are ready to be noticed.

EVERY MISTAKE MATTERS

PLACING YOUR BETS

You will bet on people and be disappointed, but don't stop believing in people all together. Just be smarter about who you bet on next time.

ONE NOTE NELLY

Don't be a one-dimensional leader in a multi-dimensional world.

LOOSE LIPS SINK CAREERS

Get the rep as someone who can always be trusted with critical info.

HEY, WHEN ABOUT ME?

You will face disappointment. How you handle it will determine your career.

GROUP GUIDE

Why read this book as a group? Because blind spots can be scary. You think you see everything and then all of a sudden, out of nowhere, something appears. I am not just talking about the kind that happen in your car. Blind spots can also happen in your career. If you want to avoid them, you need a few honest comrades to give you feedback on the things you cannot see in yourself. That is the power of a group study session.

You also can use this group to brainstorm ideas related to each chapter. It is always helpful to collaborate when thinking of strategies and responses to what you read. An executive once described this as 1 + 1 = 3. You take two ordinary people. They come together and out comes something better than either individual could have produced solo. So, share liberally, steal ideas shamelessly and help each other flush out seedlings that can be turned into full blown, knock-it-outa-the-park, career strategies.

On my website I have a Group Guide that shows you how to divide the book up into 6 weekly discussions. Visit ReaganCannon.com to download it free!